No Time to Lose

Ann Weil

Illustrated by Matthew Trueman

STECK-VAUGHN
Harcourt Supplemental Publishers

www.steck-vaughn.com

ISBN 0-7398-7533-7

Copyright © 2004 Steck-Vaughn, a division of Harcourt Supplemental Publishers, Inc. All rights reserved. No part of the material protected by this copyright may be reproduced or utilized in any form or by any means, electronic or mechanical, including photocopying, recording, or by any information storage and retrieval system, without permission in writing from the copyright owner. Requests for permission to make copies of any part of the work should be mailed to: Copyright Permissions, Steck-Vaughn, P.O. Box 26015, Austin, Texas 78755.

Power Up! Building Reading Strength is a trademark of Steck-Vaughn.

Printed in China.

2 3 4 5 6 7 8 9 M 07

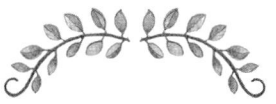

Contents

Chapter 1
The Big News 1

Chapter 2
Point of No Return 6

Chapter 3
A Whole New World 15

Chapter 4
Let the Games Begin 27

Chapter 5
A Hero's Welcome 36

Chapter 1
The Big News

Milo sat under an olive tree on the highest hill on the island. He was trying to study. The morning's lesson had been very difficult. There was a lot to memorize.

Books were rare and expensive. Very few students had enough money to buy them. Instead, the teacher read aloud while students took notes to memorize later.

Milo closed his eyes. He repeated a few sentences exactly as his teacher had spoken them that morning.

"Are you talking in your sleep?" A voice out of nowhere surprised Milo. He opened his eyes and saw his friend Pindar in front of him.

1

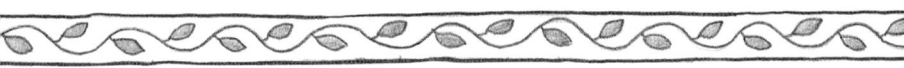

"I'm not sleeping—I'm studying," Milo said. "Maybe you should try it."

"I won't have time this summer," replied Pindar. "Didn't you hear the news?"

"What news?"

"A messenger came to the island early this morning," Pindar said as he sat down. His eyes sparkled with excitement. "He said that the Great Games are going to be held just two months from now!"

"Did the messenger bring any *important* news?" Milo picked up a tree branch that had fallen on the ground. He used it to draw circles in the dirt at his feet.

"Don't tell me you haven't heard of the Great Games. They're only held once every four years. People travel from all over Greece to compete in them."

"Of course I've heard of the Great Games, Pindar," Milo said. "I just don't see what's so 'great' about them."

"Well, everyone else thinks they're great. Kallias and Ariston are training for boxing. I think running is better than boxing, so I've decided to win that event instead."

Milo smiled. His friend Pindar had a lot of confidence in himself.

"Training by myself isn't much fun, though," Pindar continued. "That's why I've decided that you should train with me. Then we can run at the Great Games together."

"You decided that?" Milo asked. "You forget one thing, my friend. I like to exercise my brain, not my body. Seriously, Pindar, I'm not an athlete. The Great Games are for people like Ariston, Kallias, and you. I'd never win, so why bother? Now if you don't mind, I'd like to finish memorizing today's lesson."

"Is that part of your lesson, too?" Pindar pointed to some letters Milo had scratched in the dirt. They spelled the name "Cassandra." Milo quickly tried to rub out the letters with his foot, but Pindar had already read them.

"I didn't realize that you were learning about Cassandra this morning," Pindar said with a smile. "You're right—I don't pay enough attention to the teacher." Then he turned and ran down the hill.

Milo was too embarrassed to argue anyway. Cassandra was a girl who lived near him. He had written her name in the dirt in front of Pindar without realizing it.

Cassandra sometimes sat with Milo in the afternoon while he studied. She was smart and pretty, and she had a very good memory. Milo had to learn poems by a famous Greek poet named Homer. Cassandra already knew most of Homer's poems by heart. She spoke them aloud to Milo so he would remember them.

Milo loved listening to Cassandra's voice. It was as soft as a light breeze. Sometimes she put Homer's poems to music that she made up herself. Milo found that it was much easier to remember the words with the music. He really wished Cassandra were sitting beside him now.

Milo was still thinking about Cassandra when Pindar came racing back up the hill.

"Hurry, Milo!" he yelled. "Cassandra's family's boat is being blown out to sea! She was in it when a huge wave crashed over it!"

Chapter 2
Point of No Return

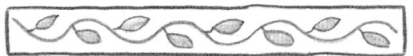

Milo jumped up and ran down the hill. He raced past Pindar, his feet barely touching the ground. Milo reached the beach and looked toward the horizon, but he didn't see any boats out on the water.

"Oh, no! I must be too late." Milo sank down on the sand and put his head in his hands. "Cassandra is lost at sea."

"Hello, Milo." Cassandra's voice caught him by surprise. Milo's heart jumped.

"What are you doing here?" he asked. "I thought you were lost at sea."

"Why would you think that? I'm on my way to help my father on his boat."

Cassandra pointed toward the beach. The boat was pulled up on the sand behind a pile of rocks. "Father was on the mainland selling pottery. I'm bringing some of the pots back home. He's letting me help make pots now. He says my work sells as well as his own does."

"That's great," said Milo.

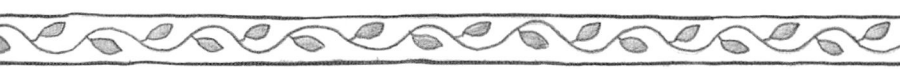

Cassandra noticed that Milo was out of breath. "Have you been running?" she asked. "Don't tell me you're training for the Great Games like the rest of those crazy boys are doing. It's hot enough without running in the heat. I thought you were smarter than that."

Milo felt silly. He didn't know what to say. He turned around when he heard Pindar's voice. Pindar was never at a loss for words.

"Running is the most ancient of all Greek sports. It's an important part of our history," said Pindar. He didn't let anyone insult his chosen sport. "Anyone who runs also knows how much fun it is."

"I'm sorry, Pindar," replied Cassandra. "I didn't mean to insult you. Are you going to compete in the Great Games, too?"

"I accept your apology," Pindar said with a smile. "Milo accepts it, too. Right, Milo? He

and I will be running in the Games together. Of course, Milo will have to settle for second place behind me. That's nothing to be ashamed of, though."

"I'm not—" Milo started to say.

"Yes, you are!" Pindar insisted. "Now if you'll excuse us, Cassandra, we have to start our training."

"No, we don't. I mean—" Milo wished the earth would open up and swallow Pindar. He was making everything worse.

"Okay then," Cassandra said. "Goodbye, Pindar. Goodbye, Milo."

Milo watched her walk away. When she was too far away to hear them, he turned to Pindar and said angrily, "You didn't have to be so rude to her. Why did you lie to me, anyway? Cassandra's boat wasn't blown away. You made me look like a fool!"

"If you'd seen how fast you ran, you'd be thanking me instead." Pindar put his hand on his friend's shoulder. Milo brushed it away.

"You tricked me," Milo said. "You just wanted to see how fast I could run."

Pindar nodded. "That's true. I wanted to show you that you could compete with the best runners, and I did. Now you have no excuse not to join me at the Great Games."

"I don't want to go," Milo said. "I would really prefer to do other things."

"What do you mean by 'other things'?" Pindar asked.

Milo paused for a few seconds. "Well, I'd prefer to study." Milo didn't tell Pindar that his studies might include sitting in the shade next to Cassandra. *Besides, Cassandra thinks that running is stupid,* he thought. *She might not like me if I compete at the Great Games.*

Pindar became serious. "Listen, I don't want to go to the Games by myself. I've never been

away from home before. You and I are like brothers. Please, Milo, I want you to come with me."

Milo wasn't used to seeing this side of Pindar. His friend was always so sure of himself. Now Pindar was asking for a favor.

Before Milo knew what he was saying, he agreed. "Okay, I'll do it, Pindar. I'll run in the Great Games with you."

Pindar's face broke into a big smile. "Great! Now we need to get you into better shape. We only have two months. That's not a lot of time to strengthen those muscles. Come on, I'll race you to the top of the hill." Pindar took off, and Milo followed him.

"Hurry up, turtle," Pindar teased. Milo ran faster, but the hill was steep. His lungs burned, and his legs ached. Sweat dripped down his forehead and stung his eyes.

Pindar was on his way down the hill when Milo reached the top. "You're lucky our race is on flat ground," Pindar shouted. "If it were uphill, you'd never make it!"

Milo ran slowly down the hill. His legs felt like water. Milo was already sorry he had said he'd race in the Great Games.

Pindar called to Milo to follow him uphill again, but Milo had run enough for one day. He walked back to the beach and looked for Cassandra, but she and her father had left.

There was no one on the beach. Milo waded out into the water. Then he started to swim. He loved spending time alone in the sea. His mind felt free as his body moved through the warm salt water.

Milo's mind wandered to the Great Games. He pictured Pindar accepting the crown of olive leaves worn by the winners. When Milo tried to picture himself in the Games, he saw nothing. He couldn't even imagine himself running the race, much less winning it. He was good at things like memorizing his lessons and swimming, but those things hardly made him a great athlete.

Milo swam harder and faster. His body sliced through the water like a sailing ship riding the wind. Even though Milo had second thoughts about training, he wouldn't go back on his word. He might not be an athlete, but he was a person of honor.

He swam until the sun touched the horizon. The clouds in the sky glowed pink. Then he got out of the water and headed home for dinner with his family. They would be very surprised by his decision. He was going to run in the Great Games.

Chapter 3
A Whole New World

The next two months passed quickly. Pindar and Milo trained together every day. They ran up and down the hill until Milo felt sick to his stomach. One day they ran around the entire island. It took them almost two hours.

Sometimes Milo felt like he couldn't run another step, but Pindar encouraged him to keep going. Milo kept running, even though he was tired. Soon he found that he could run as well as Pindar without feeling as though he was about to faint. This gave Milo confidence, and soon he was actually looking forward to the Great Games.

Milo liked to swim after he was finished running with Pindar. Swimming helped loosen his aching leg muscles, and it was also a chance to look for Cassandra along the beach. She was almost never there when he was, though.

Most people on the island were proud of the boys who were going to compete in the Great Games. Cassandra was different. She never asked Milo about his training or even mentioned the Games. *Maybe she just doesn't care about me,* he thought. Milo hoped that wasn't true.

Milo swam longer and farther now than he had before he started training. He also noticed that his leg muscles were getting larger and tighter. Milo could see and feel his body strengthening.

Maybe I am becoming an athlete, he thought to himself. It didn't make him feel any better, though. Cassandra liked poets, not athletes. Milo didn't think one person could be both.

The day came for Milo and Pindar to go to the Great Games. They met at the beach early in the morning and joined their friends Kallias and Ariston.

A crowd of people had come down to the beach to wish the athletes good luck. Milo looked around before getting into the boat to the mainland. He had hoped that Cassandra would come, but she was nowhere in sight.

Maybe she's on her way, he thought. *I'll wait another minute, just in case.*

"Hurry up," Pindar called. "You'll come in last for sure if you're this slow in the race."

Milo helped push the boat off the sand, and then he hopped into the boat. The wind was strong. Soon the island disappeared from view.

A few hours passed before the four athletes reached the mainland. Then the boat continued along the coast toward the stadium where the Great Games would be held.

Pindar slept most of the way, but Milo was too nervous to rest. He felt as though he had butterflies in his stomach. He hadn't been able to eat breakfast. It was almost time for lunch, but Milo was still not hungry.

To pass the time, Kallias and Ariston talked about boxing. Milo tried to remember some of Homer's poems, but he had forgotten them all. He thought about Cassandra instead as he listened to Pindar snore.

Pindar woke up just as the boat landed on the shore. He stretched his arms and yawned. Crowds of people were already there for the Great Games. Milo had never seen so many people before, and the scene fascinated him.

"Come on, Milo." Pindar pushed him ahead. "Let's go and see who we'll be running against tomorrow."

Pindar spent the next several hours talking to people, but Milo slipped away and went to the building where the athletes were spending the night. He wanted to get some sleep. The sun was low in the sky, and he was exhausted.

Milo woke up at dawn. He had slept well, but his body felt stiff. He decided to go for a run to loosen up his muscles before the race. As he walked outside, he saw Pindar, Ariston, and Kallias. The three friends had been awake all night.

"Why did you leave so early?" Kallias asked. "You missed a great party."

"I needed to get some sleep," Milo said. "Aren't you tired? You haven't forgotten that our race is today, have you?"

"Of course not, but there's still plenty of time for sleep," replied Pindar. "Our race doesn't start until this afternoon." He lay down in the shade of a large fig tree and closed his eyes. He had begun to snore by the time Kallias and Ariston had settled down to sleep.

Milo left them and started to run. It was early in the day, but merchants were already setting up tables in the center of town. They were selling colorful and exotic objects.

Milo wanted to buy a present for Cassandra. He saw a merchant selling small bottles of perfume, and he bought one.

"Where are you from, young man?" asked the merchant.

Milo told him, and they talked for a few minutes. As they spoke, several people walked by and waved to the merchant. He introduced Milo to one of them—a man named Strabo. Strabo had several books under his arm.

"Strabo, my friend Milo is here to run in this afternoon's race," said the merchant. "It's his first time away from home."

Strabo smiled and looked at Milo. "I can remember my first Great Games," he said. "I was about your age."

"Strabo competed in wrestling," the merchant explained to Milo. "He won every single match."

"That was a long time ago," Strabo said. "Now I spend more of my time writing than wrestling."

Milo looked at the books that Strabo was carrying. His name was on most of the covers.

"You're a real scholar, aren't you?" Milo asked with wide eyes.

"You seem surprised," Strabo said. "Many athletes enjoy books and sports equally. It's entirely possible to have both a strong body and a strong mind. In fact, the two often go together."

Milo listened as Strabo and the merchant talked about Strabo's new book. Then the two men started talking about wrestling. Several other men stopped to join the conversation.

Milo realized that many of the men were both athletes and scholars. *There's got to be a way for me to be both, too,* he thought.

Milo said goodbye and went to find some breakfast. He spent the rest of the morning seeing the sights and meeting people from all over Greece. He was fascinated by their lives in other cities and villages. Milo learned that the people from the city of Sparta spent their youth training for war, while Greeks in Athens enjoyed the arts. He decided that he would try to travel someday to see some of these exotic cities with his own eyes.

This really is an adventure, Milo thought as he walked to the stadium for his race. *Now I'm glad that Pindar asked me to come to the Great Games with him.*

Milo arrived at the stadium early, so he sat on the ground to watch the jumping contest.

The jumping pit was about fifty feet long. The athletes held heavy weights as they ran and leaped from the starting point. They swung their arms as they flew through the air. Then they threw the weights out behind them just before they landed.

The crowd cheered loudly when one boy jumped much farther than the others. He was clearly the winner. Milo tried to imagine how that boy felt. *It must be wonderful to win at the Great Games,* he thought. *Maybe my chance will come someday, too.*

The running race was starting soon. Milo looked around for Pindar. He froze when a different face caught his attention. Milo was astonished. Was it really Cassandra he had just seen? Was she really there at the Great Games?

Milo blinked. The glare of the sun blinded him for a second. When he opened his eyes again, the person who looked like Cassandra was gone.

I must have imagined that, Milo thought, shaking his head. He looked for Pindar again. *If he doesn't get here soon, he'll miss the race!*

Chapter 4
Let the Games Begin

Milo walked slowly through the crowd of spectators in search of Pindar. What he saw was Cassandra's face instead, and this time there was no mistaking her. She smiled as she walked toward him.

"Cassandra!" Milo cried. *Did she come this far just to watch me run?* he wondered.

"Hi, Milo," said Cassandra. "I thought I'd wish you good luck before your race."

"I didn't know you were coming to the Great Games," Milo said.

"I'm here with my father," Cassandra replied. "He wanted to see the Games, and he also thought it would be a good place to sell our pots."

"Are you going to watch me run?" asked Milo nervously.

Cassandra shrugged. "We have a lot to sell, so I might be too busy working."

Milo sighed with relief. At least he didn't have to worry about losing in front of her.

"I really would like to watch you run, though, so I'll do my best to see the race," she continued.

Milo was speechless. Cassandra sounded very sincere as always, and the idea that she might watch him race made him feel eight times more nervous than he already was!

"By the way, where's Pindar?" Cassandra asked. "Shouldn't he be here by now?" She pointed to several runners walking toward the starting line. Pindar wasn't among them.

"Runners, take your places," a voice called.

"You'd better go. Good luck!" Cassandra smiled at Milo and walked away.

Milo ran to the starting line. Now he had something new to worry about—Cassandra! Milo knew Cassandra didn't like athletes, but she probably liked winners more than losers. Most people did. What if he came in last? What would she think of him then?

He never should have let Pindar talk him into racing, but it was too late. He couldn't walk away because quitting was even worse than losing. Cassandra would never respect someone who quit.

Milo took his place at the starting line. Then he heard Pindar shout his name. He turned and saw his friend running toward him.

"On your marks, get set, go!"

Milo and the other runners took off a second before Pindar crossed the starting line. Pindar had made it just in time, but he looked as though he had already run three races. His hair was dripping with sweat, and he was short of breath.

Pindar caught up to Milo, and the two boys ran side by side. "I woke up... late," Pindar said between puffs of air. "I had to ... run all the way here... to make it in time."

Milo saw that his friend was too exhausted to run his best. Milo started to slow down.

"No, don't stay with me.... Go and win this race... for both of us!" Pindar gasped.

"Pindar, I don't—"

"Run, Milo!" Pindar yelled.

Milo could tell that his friend no longer had enough breath to speak, so he didn't argue. He felt sad as he ran ahead of Pindar. Then Milo thought of Cassandra. Was she watching him? Milo picked up speed. Maybe winning at the Great Games would win her respect.

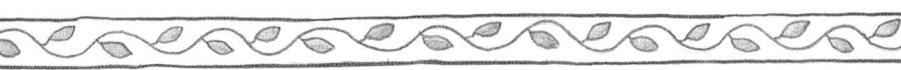

Pindar was right on Milo's heels as they finished the first lap around the stadium. There were six more laps to go. Milo's feet barely touched the ground as he ran. When he felt himself getting tired, he pushed himself harder. He didn't want to think about running out of energy before he got to the finish line. The stadium was packed with hundreds of roaring spectators, but Milo didn't hear them. He put all his energy into running as fast as he possibly could.

There were five runners ahead of Milo as he started his third lap. Some of the runners were beginning to slow down. Milo could hear their heavy breathing and see their tired faces as he caught up to them.

Milo's legs felt as though they were on fire. Sweat rolled down his face. He didn't think any training could have prepared him for this.

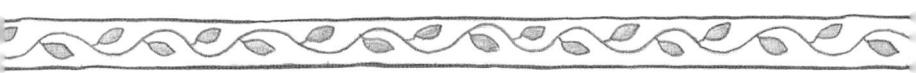

He was doing better than he thought, though. There were only three runners ahead of him by the fifth lap. Milo looked over his shoulder. Pindar was still right behind him. Milo knew that if his friend hadn't woken up so late, he'd be far ahead.

Milo passed one of the runners at the start of the seventh and final lap. Cheering fans rushed by in a big blur. Now there were only two runners ahead of him.

Milo's thoughts turned to Cassandra again. He couldn't see her, but he could almost feel her eyes on him as he ran. For some strange reason, it didn't make him nervous. Maybe all of the encouraging words from Pindar and Cassandra had pushed him this far. Milo thought about how long he had trained, and he realized that his own hard work had helped get him here, too.

Milo ran harder than he thought possible. He passed one of the two front runners with half a lap to go. Now there was only one person between him and the finish line.

Milo wanted to win. He wanted to win for Pindar. He wanted to win for Cassandra. Most of all, Milo wanted to win for himself.

With his last drop of energy, Milo dashed toward the finish line. For a moment, the crowd was silent. The race was so close that fans weren't sure who had won.

Milo knew the truth. He had felt the front runner's arm brush past his shoulder as they crossed the finish line together. The other runner had won, and Milo was second. The two athletes shook hands.

To everyone's surprise, Pindar had come in fourth. He fell to the ground after he crossed the finish line. Milo rushed over to his friend. Someone brought them water to drink.

"Are you all right?" Milo asked.

Pindar wet his lips with water and nodded. "You did well, Milo," he said. "I told you that second place is nothing to be ashamed of."

Milo looked around him, and what he saw was amazing. The spectators were going wild. He realized that they were not only cheering for the winner—they were also cheering for him.

Chapter 5
A Hero's Welcome

When Milo and Pindar returned home, there was a big party in their honor. Everyone on the island came to congratulate them. Kallias and Ariston were there, too. Even though they had not won first place in the boxing event, they had done very well. They were already thinking about competing again in four years.

Cassandra came to the party with her family. It was the first time Milo had seen her since she had wished him luck before his race. He still wasn't sure if she had been able to watch him run or not. Milo gave Cassandra the perfume he had bought for her. "I hope you like it," he said.

Cassandra smelled the perfume and sighed softly. "It's wonderful," she said. As usual, she sounded very sweet and sincere. "Thank you so much. I have a present for you, too." She handed Milo a small book of Homer's poems.

Milo was speechless. He wasn't sure he could accept such an expensive gift, but Cassandra gently insisted.

"I traded some of my pots to buy the book, so I really want you to have it," she said.

"Thank you," Milo said, taking the book. "It's beautiful."

Pindar walked over to them, and Milo quickly hid the book behind his back. He didn't want to share this special moment with Pindar. His friend was so busy telling everyone about the Great Games that he didn't even notice Milo's book.

"You should have been there, Cassandra," Pindar said. He put his arm around Milo's shoulder. "Milo ran a good race, thanks to me. I was right behind him the whole way."

"Why weren't you in front of him?" Cassandra asked.

"Well, that's a long story," Pindar said.

"We have time," replied Cassandra. She smiled at Milo.

As always, Pindar was not at a loss for words. "Well, just before our race started, a horse broke loose from its chariot," he said.

"The horse went wild and ran into the crowd. I had to rescue several small children in its path. Then I leaped onto the horse's back. It reared up onto its back legs. It tried to throw me off, but I held on to it."

"The horse finally realized it was no match for me, so it calmed down," Pindar continued. "I returned it to its grateful owner. I also fixed its owner's chariot. That's why I was so late getting to the race."

Milo looked at Cassandra. He wondered if she believed Pindar's story.

"I ran fast enough to catch up to the front runners," Pindar said. "I could have passed all of them easily, but it didn't seem fair. I was already a hero of the Great Games for saving those children's lives. It only seemed fair for someone else to get some glory, too."

As Pindar moved on to tell his story to someone else, Cassandra laughed. "Kallias told me that Pindar had just woken up too late," she said. "He didn't mention anything about 'glory.' I guess Kallias got it wrong."

After the party, Milo walked Cassandra home. There was no need for conversation. Just being with Cassandra made Milo happy.

Cassandra broke the silence. "I feel as though I owe you an apology," she said.

"For what?" Milo asked, surprised.

"I'm sorry I said all those bad things about running while you were training for the Great Games," she replied. "I'm glad I stayed to watch you run."

Milo froze. She had watched the race after all! Then the astonished look on his face melted into a smile.

"I'm glad you stayed, too," said Milo.

When Milo was alone that night, he opened the book of poems Cassandra had given him. She had written a few words to him inside the front cover. "For Milo, my favorite scholar *and* athlete."

Milo read one of the poems and then closed the book. He thought about the words that Cassandra had written to him. He remembered what Strabo had said about having both a strong mind and a strong body. Milo decided that he would work harder to have both of those things.

Milo closed his eyes. As he drifted off to sleep, he imagined he had just finished another race at the Great Games. Cassandra was there to congratulate him and place a crown of olive leaves on his head. Milo didn't have to look down at his feet to know that he was standing on top of the world.

The real Great Games were called the Olympics. They began in Greece in 776 B.C. Every four years, athletes from all over Greece would come to the stadium in the city of Olympia and compete. Greek cities, which were often at war, stopped fighting during the Olympics. This was so athletes could travel safely to and from the games.

The first Olympic Games had only one event—running across the stadium once. Over time, the number of events grew to include longer running races, boxing, wrestling, horse racing, jumping, and throwing.

Only men who spoke Greek could compete in these events. The winners brought fame to their towns. Many of these athletes are still famous today, over two thousand years later!